GET UP, GET OUT, AND GO!
Unleash Your Inner Girl: The Journey to Courage, Joy and Self-Discovery

Sunnie Givens

Sunny House

Copyright © 2015 by Sunny House

All rights reserved. This book or any portion thereof may not be reproduced or used in any manner whatsoever without the express written permission of the publisher except for the use of brief quotations in a book review or scholarly journal.

First Printing: 2015

ISBN -10: 0989506312

Sunny House
3839 McKinney Avenue
#155-765
Dallas, Texas 75204
www.sunniegivens.com

Ordering Information:

Special discounts are available on quantity purchases by corporations, associations, educators, and others. For details, contact the publisher at the above listed address.

U.S. trade bookstores and wholesalers: Please contact Sunnie Givens via email at sunnie@sunniegivens.com. You can also find me on Facebook at https://www.facebook.com/sunniegiv.

Dedication

To the courageous women, who have yet to find their wings and experience the true freedom that courage brings; To the joyful women, overworked, super busy and multi-tasking, who have a strong desire to explore the world. May you find confidence within to replace the validation you have been seeking elsewhere. To live the life you truly desire start by rewriting your own story of happiness.

To the women of Joyful Living Community, thank you for shining your light so brightly that others want to know you. May we continue to express charisma and guide the world through philanthropic opportunities.

Table of Contents

Acknowledgements 8

Welcome! 9

Chapter 1: The Secret 12

Journal Exercise: Letter to My Fear 19

Journal Exercise: Letter to Courage 21

Contract with Myself 22

Chapter 2: The Girl Who Traveled the World 25

A Lesson in Forgiveness 30

A Lesson in the Power of the Human Spirit 33

A Lesson in the Joy of Spontaneity 35

A Lesson in Finding Joy and Laughter in
   the Oddest Places 38

A Lesson in the Closeness of What is Most Treasured 41

A Lesson in Molten Cake 44

Travel Photos 48

Journal Exercise: Dream a Little 58

Journal Exercise: Technology Free 59

Chapter 3: Turning Dreams into Reality 62

Map of Sunnie's World Travel 68

Traveling Solo 71

Falling on Fifth Avenue 75

Journal Exercise: Visioning 79

Chapter 4: Inner Girl Issues 81

Journal Exercise: Food For Thought 86

Journal Exercise: Unleash Your Inner Girl 87
Personal Stories 89
Sunnie in the City 93
About the Author 97
Notes 101

Acknowledgements

To Mo, thank you for your support and encouragement.

To my editor, Lorna Johnson, for all of the fun times we had putting this book together;

To Theresa Campbell for the beautiful design and layout of this book.

To the inner girl inside of me who bravely lives each day in full gratitude of a life well lived;

To my children and grandchildren for always letting me know how proud they are of me, and for being the biggest joy in my life…

I thank you.

Welcome!

People ask me this all of the time – how I live with such courage and zest for life. Why I'm not afraid to walk up to a stranger on a street in Paris or Brazil and strike up a conversation.

Its curiosity and charisma! Curiosity and charisma will take you on adventures, whether you're in your hometown or in Argentina. And, the woman who taught me all about charisma is my adoptive Mom. She was the ultimate "Get Up, Get Out and Go" girl. I learned absolutely everything from watching her, from being with her.

I'm so grateful for her example, for her sense of spirit and adventure. And I hope to pass on some of that to you!

Joyfully,

Sunnie Givens

"There is no end to the adventures we can have if only we seek them with our eyes open."

Jawaharlal Nehru

Chapter 1
THE SECRET

Chapter 1: The Secret

The Ultimate Get Up, Get Out and Go, Girl!

"How do you do it?"

People ask me how I live with such courage and zest for life and why I'm not afraid to walk up to a stranger on a street in Salvador, Brazil and strike up a conversation. Its charisma and courage, which will take you on adventures, whether you're in your hometown or in Costa Rica.

And the woman who taught me everything I know? My Mom, Addie, who adopted me when I was eleven. She was the ultimate "Get Up, Get Out and Go Girl," and I learned everything from watching her. I'm so grateful for her example, for her sense of spirit and adventure.

I wrote this book because I hope to pass on some of that to you.

When I was a teenager, my Mom would take me to the heart of downtown Chicago to her favorite restaurant. We would walk in to find a long line of people waiting to get seated, but my Mom and I would get ushered to a table immediately.

I always wondered, "How is it we got a seat so quickly? And why is everyone so excited to see her?"

Through my observations over the years, I learned that my Mom's secret was how she made everyone feel. She tipped generously, and her energy was electric. She connected with everyone and laughed and joked with them as if they were close friends. And guess who does that now? I have been seated at restaurants in Paris and Washington D.C. that had over two-hour waits all due to having a magnetic, joyful personality.

In all the years my Mom was alive, I don't think I ever saw her sad.

She had perfected the art of joyful living by always keeping the spirit of her inner girl alive.

And she taught me how to do the same.

She inspired me to live my life to the fullest, taught me the importance of sisterhood, and how to live each Moment as an adventure. I was mesmerized by her euphoric charisma.

My Mom had five wonderful girlfriends. They lived in Chicago and we lived in the suburbs. My Mom was a city girl at heart. They all went out so often, I began to get curious as to where she was going.

She was a night owl. After her children went to sleep, my Mom transformed herself in to a glamorous woman that was ready to hit the town. It didn't matter if it was a weeknight or not. She did not have restrictions placed on her life based on what our society thought she should, or should not do as a mother.

I remember one night when I was a teenager, my Mom was listening to jazz, drinking champagne, and getting dressed to go out with her friends like she always did. I really wanted to go with her. Finally, she agreed to take me and I got dressed in what I thought was a nice outfit.

My Mom took one look at what I picked out and promptly gave me a makeover – a pencil skirt, a Sophia Loren blouse and t-strapped pumps.

She took me to various cultural events that night but my favorite place was the jazz club. I could not believe my Mom allowed me to accompany her with her girlfriends. Imagine being a teenager hanging with your amazing mother and using a car service to take you from place to place. It was magical! I watched Mom laugh with her friends, listen to her favorite music, request songs she loved, and dance the night away. I was mesmerized by her and by her incredible charisma.

She took me with her many times over the years, and from her influence I learned to love different cultures, food, music, the arts and fashion. She laughed and talked with anyone, and before you knew it, everyone would be sitting at our table. I watched her with admiration thinking, *"She chose me to be her daughter!"* She was not like the other Moms and I was proud.

These were the times she let her inner girl out to play, and I'm so grateful I was shown how to keep my own good-natured spirit alive as I grew up. Through her example, I learned how to live with no regrets, to live like a woman and play like a girl.

I've been on incredible adventures. As I look back on the places I have been, the people I met, and the memories I made, I feel blessed to have had my mother as my example of how to live with charisma and travel courageously.

And now I'm here to be that for you.

To live with charisma means that you live your life out loud and on your own terms. It means that you follow your passions and stand up for what you value and believe in.

TO TRAVEL COURAGEOUSLY MEANS YOU'RE NOT AFRAID TO BOOK A TRIP AND GO, EVEN IF NO ONE IS WILLING TO TRAVEL WITH YOU.

It also means you won't be solo for long anyway, because you'll become one of those magnetic women who never meets a stranger, and who gets invited to cultural events, active adventures, dinners with new friends… you name it!

Living in this manner means changing your entire mindset from one of fear to courage and playfulness.

And even though I was blessed with a very charismatic mother, I still had to deal with some of my own fears when it came time for me to stretch and move beyond my limits and create the life of my dreams.

As I moved into adulthood and a life of responsibility, motherhood, career and being a wife, I didn't want to lose touch with the lightheartedness of my own inner girl. I was afraid that if I let her express herself fully, I would be rejected or not taken seriously.

For instance, my inner girl loves to sing.

It's one of my dreams to sing in front of an audience like I did as a child. As an adult, I struggled with stage fright. It's something I'm just starting to get over. I constantly meditate on times in my life when I chose courage over fear and I'm determined to get on stage and let my inner girl spirit flow.

My point? Our dissatisfaction with our life is because we have put our inner girl in a "time-out." The way to get out of a "time-out" is to find the courage to manage your fear and have those experiences that you secretly dream of.

Over the next few pages, I'm going to share with you some exercises that helped me shift my entire outlook from fearful to joyful living.

Then, in Chapter Two, I'll share with you the wonderful adventures that happened as a result of my shift. They are unpredictable, life-changing stories from my travels, and they're meant to inspire you to create your own exuberant adventures.

My wish is to show you what is truly possible when you shed your fear and commit to living life to the fullest, so that the next time your girlfriends ask you if you can come out to play, your answer will be, "Yes!"

Next time you get a fabulous offer say, Yes!

The only thing stopping you from living your life courageously is fear. And as I said, it's something I am still working through as well. In fact, we never really overcome it; we learn to choose courage instead. How do you do that? You've got to confront your fear head on and acknowledge the power it has had over your life.

I did this by writing a letter to my fear, asking it why it was chattering in my ear, telling me lies about my ability to accomplish my dreams. Through this, I became aware of the power it had over me.

Then I wrote another letter, this time determining that from now on, I would choose to live according to my core passions which takes courage.

MAKE THE SHIFT FROM FEAR TO COURAGE.

In this letter, I let my courage take over to write, "Dear Fear, I welcome you, I notice you and I hear you. I want to inform you that you will no longer be guiding my life. Courage will take over now." It was a powerful and necessary exercise, and I encourage you to do the same.

Live freely.

Journal Exercises

Journal Exercise: Letter to My Fear

Exercise One

One of the things I'll be asking you to do is to keep a journal as you read this book. Each chapter will include thought-provoking questions that will inspire, challenge and uplift you.

The first journal exercise I want you to do is write your own letter to your fear just like I've done.

Here are some questions that will help prompt your writing.

Letter to Your Fear

1. In the past, what ways has your fear held you back from realizing your dreams?

2. What places would you travel to if you decided today not to listen to your fear?

3. What dreams and goals are you most afraid of achieving or experiencing now?

Letter to Your Courage

1. List five (5) things you would do this year if you had the courage to do so?

2. If you do not live courageously now, how will your inner girl suffer?

3. If you had the courage, how could you positively impact the lives of others?

Write as long as you need to in order to get all the fears out on the page and to really, truly explore what it means for you to live a life of courage.

Journal Exercise: Letter to Courage

So, to keep the positive momentum going, I'd like you to now reflect on times when you have put fear to the side and chosen to act out of courage.

Do some journaling about the times in your life when you felt the fear but did it anyway, and all the positive experiences that resulted from doing so.

This is meant to help you see that you likely have more courage than you realize, and that even though it's uncomfortable to step outside your comfort zone and live fearlessly, the benefits are undeniably rewarding!

Contract with Myself

Exercise Three

The last exercise I want you to do is also the most important. You're going to write a contract with yourself that you are going to live your life from a place of courage, not of fear. Words are powerful, and making a solemn vow with yourself can be a powerful way of ensuring that you take this new outlook on life seriously.

Sample Contract:

I, _____, on this day, _____,
commit to living my life from a
place of courage, with a spirit of adventure and creativity,
no matter what. No matter who judges me.
From now on I choose to live a life of freedom and creativity.
I choose to be authentic and live my life without a single
regret. I choose a life of sisterhood and fun!
Life is unpredictable, so today I decide my life is too
precious to waste worrying what anyone will
think about how I want to live,
love and enjoy my life.
I choose to live out loud.

Signed,

_____
Your Name

Releasing my inner girl and my playfulness led me to traveling without any fear.

Next, I'll share some of my amazing adventures, which wouldn't have been possible if I hadn't let my little girl lead the way on many of them. If traveling courageously is one of your desires, my goal in sharing these stories is to inspire you to live in the moment and do the same.

So, let's go traveling! First stop… Salvador, Brazil!

Chapter 2
TRAVELING THE WORLD

Chapter 2: The Girl Who Traveled the World

Salvador, Brazil: Handy, A True Renaissance Man

There are no typical adventures. When you live life to the fullest and travel courageously, your journeys will be infused with incredible life lessons and will also bring you some of the most touching relationships and surprising experiences.

Among other things, I learned forgiveness in South Africa, experienced the power of the human spirit in Australia, found joy and laughter in a hospital emergency room in Singapore, and discovered that I enjoy the excitement in Brazil.

Here are my stories. I hope they inspire you to leave the comfort of your home and seek your own life lessons, and make lifelong relationships in exotic places.

But before I dive in, I have to tell you about Handy. This man stole my heart and touched my soul, and taught me so much about living the good life on my own terms. Handy is the perfect example of how to overcome adversity and live a life full of joy. If my Mom is my heroine, Handy is my hero. Here is the amazing story of how we met.

I flew into Rio, stayed at the Copacabana Hotel and shopped in Ipanema (remember the song, "The Girl from Ipanema"?). Yes, that one.

I did all the typical touristy activities. But what I have found time and time again is that when you do the typical stuff, typical stuff happens – meaning not much.

I was longing for experiences with spice and pizzazz.

I wanted to fly to Bahia, the largest state on the northeastern coast of Brazil. I'd heard of the Afro-Brazilians there and wanted to experience their culture, food and history.

Through a fluke of events, I found this incredible, boutique hotel called The House of Old Doors, or "A Casa das Portas Velhas," which is where I decided to stay. The owner hired a Venezuelan man to create, restore and refurbish old doors as the main focus of the hotel.

There's even a house of doors museum on the second level.

So, I walked in and to my left, sitting in the lobby was a man who looked just like my favorite uncle – bald, caramel skin, big, white teeth, large brown eyes, and round glasses.

He was wearing a forest-green, cotton, short-sleeve t-shirt with green leaves and some kind of yellow wooden symbol on it, and was sitting, legs crossed, smoking a cigarette in one of the lobby chairs. A very sophisticated, dapper-looking man. I was instantly charmed by him.

And because I never meet a stranger, I walked right over to him, struck up a conversation and we started talking up a storm. He told me he was an

American from New York, and the next thing you know, he was telling me to go change into casual evening attire and that he was going to take me for dinner and dancing on the town.

I thought I was going with another one of the hotel guests. But over the course of the night I learned that Handy was, in fact, the *owner*.

And that chair he was sitting in was his favorite smoking chair. He had flown all of his own furniture over from his New York apartment and had designed the entire hotel from the ground up. The lobby was essentially his relocated living room.

This is what I mean by living life out loud and with courage. I walked into this beautiful boutique hotel and suddenly had a dinner and dancing invitation with the owner. Imagine how uneventful my trip would have been if I did not get out of my comfort zone and talk to Handy.
But this was only the beginning of the story...

Handy took me out on the town and we danced in the street and had a wonderful time. He took my friend and me to all kinds of restaurants. At one point I told him how much I loved hospitality and he told me to just make myself at home in his hotel. "You can even go in the kitchen if you want," he offered.

So, that's what I did. The next morning I went down the back stairs into the kitchen for breakfast. I was sitting on the counter peeling potatoes with the ladies when Handy came in. "What in the world? You really made yourself at home!" he exclaimed.

I told him I was perfectly happy serving the guests and that I wanted to feel like I worked there. I finished the potatoes and joined Handy for breakfast. He told us all kinds of stories about the difficulties and the joys of building this hotel, and of living in several other countries and learning their languages and cultures.

At one point, I told him how I admired Photographer Gordon Parks, the first black photographer who worked for *Time* magazine. He told me he knew him and would be happy to introduce me one day. I also mentioned how I loved Gordon Parks' story on Flavio, who as a young child was given the opportunity to come to the United States from Brazil to have surgery. Handy told me he also knew where Flavio lived and would take me to see his house.

And he *did*.

Four days later, I left and went to Kia Roa, a remote island accessible only by private plane or boat. I didn't really want to leave, but it was on my itinerary to go there for a full week. And even though it was beautiful and I enjoyed the activities, I missed the excitement of the city.

After two days, I looked online to see if Handy had any rooms available. He was booked solid. I called the hotel anyway and asked if they knew of any hotels nearby. "I miss you guys!" I told the concierge, who promptly put Handy on the phone. "I knew you'd be bored over there," he said slyly. "I know it says I'm booked, but for you, never. I still have your room."

Of course I went straight back. I could not put my bags down quick enough before we were out dancing in the street all night. I spent the next three days there, celebrating Fat Tuesday, drinking *Caipirinhas* and watching dancers perform *capoeira*, a Brazilian martial art that combines dance, acrobatics and music.

It was time to leave the hotel. As I was putting my bags in the car, I turned around to see everyone standing outside – the *entire* hotel staff – standing in the doorway, tearful and waiting to say goodbye to me. Even the lady who did my laundry had tears in her eyes.

When I looked at Handy, surprised, he said, "I'd cry, too. You paid her rent for six months. You're a big tipper. What you think is small is big to someone else."

Handy sold the hotel and moved home to Virginia. Before he passed away, he told me he had lived an incredible life and did everything he wanted to do. He lived in foreign countries, learned their languages, started businesses, and made friends all over the world.

I have Handy's picture in my living room next to his look-a-like, my favorite Uncles Charles. They have both passed on leaving me with life-changing memories to share.

I never imagined I would meet one of the most inspirational people in my life at a boutique hotel in Salvador, Brazil.

The Lesson: Go beyond your comfort zone and explore more than the typical, touristy activities

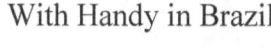

With Handy in Brazil

A Lesson in Forgiveness

South Africa

I flew to Cape Town South Africa because I wanted to visit Robben Island, Where Nelson Mandela was imprisoned. Mandela is famous for saying that South Africa belongs to everyone, even the people who had imprisoned him.

I believe this makes Mandela the ultimate forgiver. I wanted and needed to forgive my biological mom, so I thought what better place to go for healing than there.

And to see what he went through, and the very jail cell he stayed in, allowed me to finally say to my birth Mom, "I forgive you." Not for putting me up for adoption, which was the most courageous thing she did for me.

No! I was forgiving her and myself for holding on to deeply-rooted childhood pains.

It was incredibly liberating to be able to finally forgive her and move on.

There was also some amazing magic that happened to me on this trip.

I stayed for a week at Kruger National Park, where tourists visit to photograph what they call "The Big Five:" the Elephant, Lion, Leopard, Buffalo and Rhinoceros.

And these elusive animals are so hard to spot, it can take two weeks to get pictures of all of them.

Amazingly, I saw *all five* on my first day.

As soon as we came back from the safari tour, people were playing music and someone grabbed my hand and started dancing with me. I had no idea what was going on, but I certainly didn't hesitate to join in the fun.

"What's going on?!" I yelled, in between dance moves.

"We're celebrating!" they said. "You saw the Big Five!" Even people in my truck didn't see all of them. And there I was just being present and taking pictures.

THERE'S AN ELEPHANT. SNAP. THERE'S A LION. SNAP. THERE'S A LEOPARD. SNAP. THERE'S A BUFFALO. SNAP. THERE'S A RHINO. SNAP.

The Lesson: Forgiveness is powerful, and you can find it in a tiny cell, on a small island, far from home. It releases you from long-held patterns, and can free you to live your life to the fullest. I am so grateful for my experience in Cape Town because presence brings incredible blessings.

The Lesson

Forgiveness & Presence Brings Incredible Blessings.

A Lesson in the Power of the Human Spirit

Australia

I went to Australia because I wanted to visit the Aboriginal – indigenous people I had studied about in an anthropology class. I had just seen the movie, "Rabbit-Proof Fence," a true story about their unjust treatment. I wasn't content just watching their story on the big screen or studying about them in a classroom.

I wanted to experience the culture for myself. So I booked a ticket and flew to the Australian Outback.

I was sitting on a bench outside a cultural center in Ayres Rock, and noticed a bunch of little girls staring at me. So we had a contest. I smiled. They smiled. I waved. They waved. I looked their direction and then looked away.

Then I looked their direction and looked away again, and they started giggling. Finally, they came close and even touched my hair. I think they were curious because mine was similar to theirs.

We didn't speak the same language, but we didn't have to. A smile is a universal language of its own.

All of a sudden, a flood of emotions poured through me and I started crying. But they were not tears of sadness.

They were tears of joy from feeling so blessed to be in this place. Just a few weeks earlier I had been halfway across the world, watching a movie and reading textbooks about Australia's native people and their culture, and now there I was. They had come off the movie screen and out of the pages of a book and into my real life and had come alive right before my eyes.

My inner girl from Chicago was sharing a tender and silly moment with a group of giggling girls from the Outback.

A smile is a universal language all its own.

The Lesson: Take action. If you're moved by your curiosity about a culture, *act* on it!

A Lesson in the Joy of Spontaneity

Easter Island

In the middle of my two-month trek through South America, I decided to take a quick detour and travel to Easter Island.

It's one of the most remote islands in the world, so even though it was close, getting there was quite a hassle.

I wanted to go because my daughter emailed me, having just watched a captivating show on its statues, and encouraged me not to miss visiting this legendary location.

I had only planned to go for a day but while I was there, the airline cancelled my return flight, so I was able to spend two wonderful days enjoying the island's annual Tapati Festival and seeing the incredible Moai stone statues.

It was definitely worth spontaneously adding this trip to my plans.

The Tapati Festival celebrates the Rapa Nui culture – the natives of Easter Island – and includes rituals, competitions, music, dancing and the selection of the Festival Queen. It was a party both days. I stayed at a little bed and breakfast right by the ocean. Each day, I got up early in the morning, went for a walk, had breakfast and rode a bike along the beach.

I wanted to see every historic site I could, so I hired a guide and toured the island and then at night, went out to the Hanga Roa neighborhood on the waterfront to take part in the festivities.

Almost no one spoke English, but it didn't matter. We understood each other, because music, dancing, smiles and laughter are their own universal languages. At the end of one of my tours, I told my guide I was craving an empanada and he told me there was a black lady who made the best empanadas on the island. This is significant because even though she was native to the island, the typical Rapa Nui looks Polynesian, not African American.

When we arrived at her famous restaurant on the waterfront, called "Donde la Tia Sonia," it was already closing. My guide went to speak to the owner and explained we were Americans and had specifically come looking for her famous empanadas.

The owner then looked up, saw me and let out a shout of joy. She came out of the kitchen and gave me a big hug. The guide said she was so happy because she had never met another black American before.

We ended our time together with her reopening the kitchen to make us a variety of her delicious empanadas.

The Lesson

Spontaneity breeds meaningful surprises. When you deviate from your original plans, YOU can affect the environment and be impacted as well.

A Lesson in Finding Joy and Laughter in the Oddest Places

Singapore

I got sick two days after I landed in Singapore and had to go to the emergency room at St. Elizabeth Hospital.

When I entered, there was no one inside except for a few nurses. To me, this was not a good sign. I was used to American emergency rooms that were bustling and full of patients. An empty one meant it was poorly organized, in my opinion.

But it was extremely clean, so I thought maybe I was in luck and would be in good hands. A specialist came to get me and told me to squeeze his hand, maybe to check for my level of strength and see how sick I was. I really didn't know.

But what startled me is what he said next. "Soft hands, not enough work," he exclaimed.

I was having trouble understanding what the doctor was saying by this. A nurse nearby began sweeping the floor and looking at me, in an effort to help me understand what the doctor meant, "Oh, hard work!" I said, laughing and shaking my head, no.

And they all laughed.

Living outside of your comfort zone is where the beauty lies.

I think I ended up with eleven people in the room, trying to cheer me up. Someone was even massaging my feet! And on top of that, the medication they gave me ended up costing only $5.

It's amazing how well we can understand each other just from a few hand motions or facial expressions.

After the doctor took some tests, he told me I had gotten food poisoning, but not from visiting Singapore. They were very proud of their clean country and knew I couldn't have gotten sick there.

After I was done, they were so hospitable, they even wheeled me out to the taxi and everybody came outside and we all hugged.

I know it might sound crazy, but even though I visited other places in Singapore, including the Raffles Hotel, Sentosa Island by cable car, Chinatown, shopping in Clarke Quay, and visiting gorgeous Singapore Botanic Gardens, the emergency room visit was the highlight of my trip.

And I really do think I got well from all that love. How could I be sick after that wonderful foot massage and so much laughter and good-natured humor?

This was a real-life example of that famous saying,

"Laughter is the best medicine." No wonder the emergency room had no patients in it!

Who would have thought I'd find joy and laughter in an emergency room at St. Elizabeth Hospital in Singapore?

The Lesson

You can find joy and laughter in the oddest places, as long as you're open to it.

A Lesson in the Closeness of What is Most Treasured

Martha's Vineyard

When I think of Martha's Vineyard, I think of untouched beauty, of a pristine place that time has left alone.

On this island, some people say that you can leave your bike outside, or your keys in the car, and no one will steal them. There are no chain restaurants or department stores.

There is music, art and bed and breakfasts everywhere, and not to mention live jazz on the beach. Oh, how I love the gingerbread cottages in Oak Bluffs.

They were built back in the 1800s in the style of little New England homes and they look exactly like life-sized gingerbread cottages. As usual, I went because of a movie.

It was called "Inkwell."

Live life on your terms.

Back in the day, African Americans weren't allowed in the ocean in Martha's Vineyard, but they went anyway, and the residents called the area of the beach where they entered, Inkwell.

This was considered an extremely derogative term and wasn't used until recently, but now this area is a thriving place where many African Americans reside and vacation, and is host to African American film and jazz festivals. A negative experience was turned into a positive.

I also read about the many influential African Americans that called Martha's Vineyard home, including the writer, Dorothy West, who was a member of the Harlem Renaissance Group, and another black lady who owned a famous bed and breakfast called, Shearer Cottage.

And as usual, I didn't just want to read about Martha's Vineyard. I wanted to experience it for myself.

At one point, I was walking down the street and noticed a beautiful woman walking with her husband. She must have been in her 70s. I struck up a conversation with her, and she ended up inviting me to her beautiful home.

She was a complete stranger and not only welcomed me to her home, but ended up showing me around the neighborhood.

The people are so warm, friendly and open. It's amazing!

She then showed me around the island shops, and when we ended our tour and time together she said, "Sunnie, you always have a place to stay when you come here."

Although Martha's Vineyard is here in the United States, because of its unspoiled history, it has an atmosphere all of its own.

The Lesson: I've been all over the world but I didn't have to travel far from home to find the place I treasure most. It may be that *you* find the place that is most special to you, is closer than you think.

The Lesson

It may be that the
place you find
the most special to you
is closer
than you think.

A Lesson in Molten Cake

Rome, Italy

Can you guess what sent me packing to Rome? It had to have been a book, a movie or a TV program, right?

It was actually three movies. After seeing the charismatic woman herself, Miss Sophia Loren, walking down those charming streets in Italy with a dress that shouted femininity!

"In The Gold of Naples," and then again after watching "Three Coins in the Fountain" and "Roman Holiday" with Audrey Hepburn, it was impossible not to visit Rome and experience this iconic and romantic city for myself.

When I arrived, I first made a wish and threw my coins into the famous Trevi Fountain. Next, I headed to the Spanish Steps to watch the artists sitting outside with their easels sketching and painting their muse.

Fancy yourself an Italian getaway!

It was so dramatic and invigorating to be immersed in the culture of the Eternal City! The next morning, I went for a stroll in search of a lovely café to have breakfast. I wore a stylish summer dress down the seductive streets of Rome as if I was Sophia Loren in the movie "The Gold of Naples."

While I was in the café, I struck up a conversation with a few locals, who told me I just had to experience Italian opera. They invited me to go with them that night to Teatro dell'Opera Di Roma. Of course, I accepted.

Well, there was no way I was walking down cobblestone streets in my high heels, so I put on my flip flops and my gown and went to the opera.

And this leads me to the search for molten chocolate cake.

I tasted the infamous cake for the first time earlier in my trip to Venice, and when I was at my hotel in Rome, I was suddenly struck with a craving for chocolate molten cake. I didn't see it on the menu, so I asked the waiter if they had it. He said they didn't have it. But I didn't let that stop me.

I went to the kitchen and decided to ask the chef if he'd make one for me. I was like an addict and I needed my chocolate fix.

This was a five star hotel. I told the chef, "I know you can do it," and with a good-natured attitude, he agreed to try.

It turned out perfect. And instead of being disgruntled about the whole thing, the chef actually gave me a hug and said, "This is my present to you, my dear."

You can have your cake and eat it, too, literally. The lesson here is that going after what you want, whether it's on "the menu of life" or not, is good not only for *you*, but for the one who's helping you.

If you have a good-natured spirit, sprinkled with charisma and drive, you'll get what you want and inspire other people to help you get it, and everyone will be happier and more enriched in the end.

And of course, the other lesson here is to not sit at home, pining after people you see in movies living the life you want to live.

The Lesson: If you see someone you admire doing something you wish you were doing, get up, get out and go create your own inspired experience. Become your own Sophia Loren, just like I did.

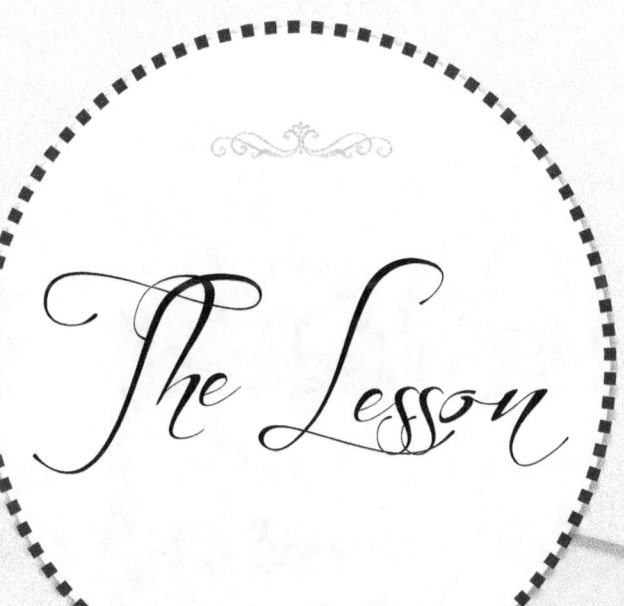

The Lesson

If you see someone you admire doing something you wish you were doing, get up, get out and go create your own inspired experience.

Travel Photos

South Africa

Elephant Riding in Thailand

Kruger National Game Park

Peru

Rome, Italy

Quito, Ecuador

Singapore

Buenos Aires, Argentina

My Mom in Chicago

Journal Exercises

So, now you've heard my stories from around the world. Hopefully you've been inspired to go create travel adventures of your own – and not in the typical touristy way, but in a way that reflects you: your personality, your spirit of adventure, your courage and charisma, and in the way you connect with and learn about other cultures.

As I've said before, this isn't only about travelling. It's about a mindset. When you see your life as an adventure and when you see an Aborigine who doesn't speak your language as both a fascinating and mysterious person you've never met before and someone who's already your best friend, you know what it means to live life to the fullest, out loud, and with no regrets and to never meet a stranger.

Because this is really what we're here to do. We're not here to live small, our faces buried in our iPhones, scurrying from one building to the next, one task to the next, until we die. We're here to live with our faces to the sky, dancing effortlessly in the streets with friends we've just met to music we've never heard because it's a universal language we know in our bones.

And that's where we're headed next. Let's make this real, for you, and in your life. In chapter three, you'll be creating your dream destination list and travel vision board, and you'll be well on your way to making adventure your new way of life.

My Trip to Easter Island

Journal Exercise: Dream a Little

Exercise One

Love of Music and Dance

I've talked about the universal languages of music and dancing and how they connect people in a powerful way.

Be swept away to another country by taking a dance lesson, like tango or salsa, or going to listen to a cumbia band or going to the opera.

What's a form of music or dancing you've never experienced that's available to you in your city or town?

_____
_____
_____
_____
_____
_____

Journal Exercise: Technology Free

You don't have to travel to an exotic country to live a life of adventure.

What can you do in your life, today, to lift your head from the glow of your laptop or iPhone screen and become present to the adventures that are available to you right now?

List Your Ideas

_____

_____

_____

_____

_____

_____

_____

_____

_____

_____

Feeding Tiger in Thailand

Chapter 3
DREAMS INTO REALITY

Chapter 3: Turning Dreams into Reality

Create a Joyful Life: Now it's Your Turn

Time to go from living vicariously through my stories to creating your own.

Time to stop wishing and to start truly living.

Time to make your dreams a reality by getting them out of your head and into your everyday life.

Time to set powerful intentions for what you deeply desire for your adventure goals, so they can come true for you.

I'm going to share with you exactly what I did – what caused me to be able to achieve travel dream after travel dream without much effort: it was the creation of a travel vision board. And if you mistake this for an arts-and-crafts project, you're missing the point.

This is a powerful manifesting, big-picture, visioning project.

MY FIRST TRAVEL VISION BOARD

I made my first board without knowing how I'd get to all the places I wanted to go or how I'd find the money to afford it, and before I knew it, I was checking off trip after trip. Sometimes I would take entire boards down at once, because I'd already quickly manifested trips to every place I'd put up. That's how powerfully this works.

I suggest that you don't think about it much and don't judge the process or approach. Just set the intention for your wildest dream destinations, create your travel vision board and believe that your adventures will happen at the right time.

Don't worry about the how – how you'll get the money, how you'll make it happen, or how you'll travel with or without the children. Just "set it and forget it" and let your vision and your new "get up, get out and go" spirit lead you to the right opportunities at the right time.

Write down all of your favorite travel destinations -- the places you've always dreamed of going. Don't worry about cost or practicality right now. Don't worry about timing. Just let your little girl have fun dreaming this list up. Then, armed with your list, create your board.

I always put a picture of myself in the middle so I'm surrounded by images of the all of the things I want to do and the places I want to experience.

When you're done, put it where you'll be sure to see it every day. I like to put mine in my bedroom or on the wall in my office. For inspiration, I've included the first list I made below. It's amazing to me that all these places were once a dream and now they're incredible, indelible memories of amazing travel.

AROUND THE WORLD

South America

- Brazil: Salvador da Bahia, San Paulo, Rio
- Argentina: Buenos Aires, Recoleta, Palermo Soho
- Chile: Santiago; Bella Vista, Easter Island
- Ecuador: Cuenca, Quito, Galapagos Island
- Peru: Lima, Cuzco, Machu Picchu
- Uruguay: Montevideo
- Colombia: Cartagena de India

Australia

- Sydney
- Melbourne
- Queensland
- Cairns
- Brisbane
- Ayres Rock

South Pacific

- New Zealand: Auckland, Waitomo
- Fiji: Viti Levu, Turtle Island
- Papua New Guinea

Asia

- China: Beijing, Shanghai
- Singapore
- Malaysia

Africa

- South Africa: Cape Town, Johannesburg, Kruger National Park, Durban
- Morocco: Casablanca

Antarctica

- Peninsula

Europe

- England
- Italy: Rome, Venice, Milan, Tuscany
- France: Paris, Nantes
- Spain: Barcelona, Madrid,
- Portugal: Lisbon
- Greece: Athens,
- Turkey: Istanbul
- Germany

North America

- Central America: Costa Rica, Panama,
- Canada: Vancouver, Victoria Island, Montreal and Toronto
- Caribbean Islands: Curacao, Bermuda and Anguilla
- United States: Travel by train across the East Coast and the West Coast

And I'm still not done. I have a travel vision board hanging in my office right now, and here are the destinations I'll be heading to next:

Asia

- Japan: Tokyo
- Hong Kong
- Thailand: Bangkok
- Indonesia: Bali
- Dubai

Africa

- Ghana: Accra
- Egypt: Luxor
- Madagascar
- Sierra Leon
- Senegal
- Tanzania
- Botswana
- Seychelles

Europe

- Scotland
- Netherlands: Amsterdam
- Denmark: Copenhagen
- Prague
- Ireland: Dublin
- Switzerland: Geneva
- Finland
- Poland

My Travel Map

Map of Sunnie's World Travels

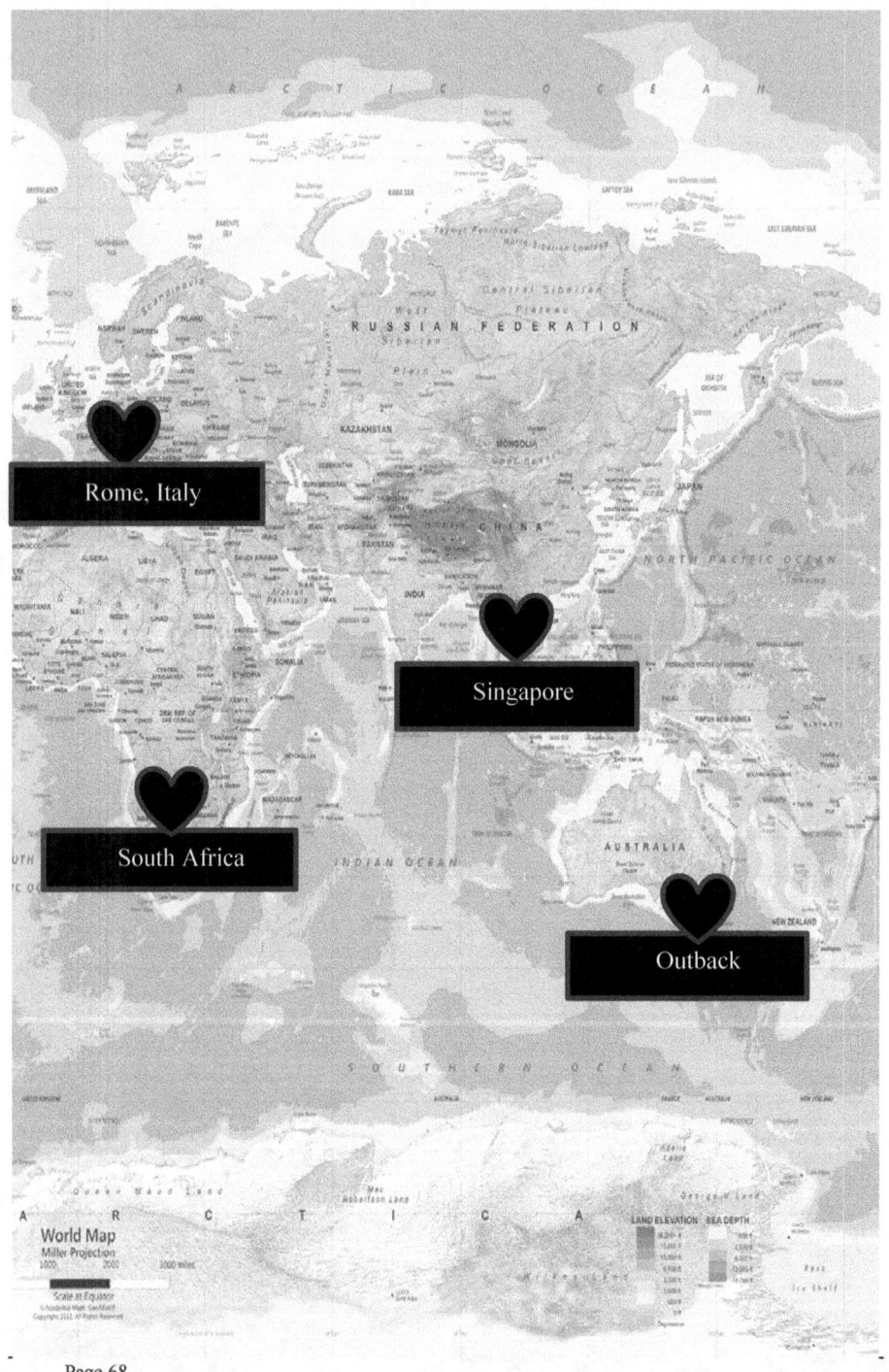

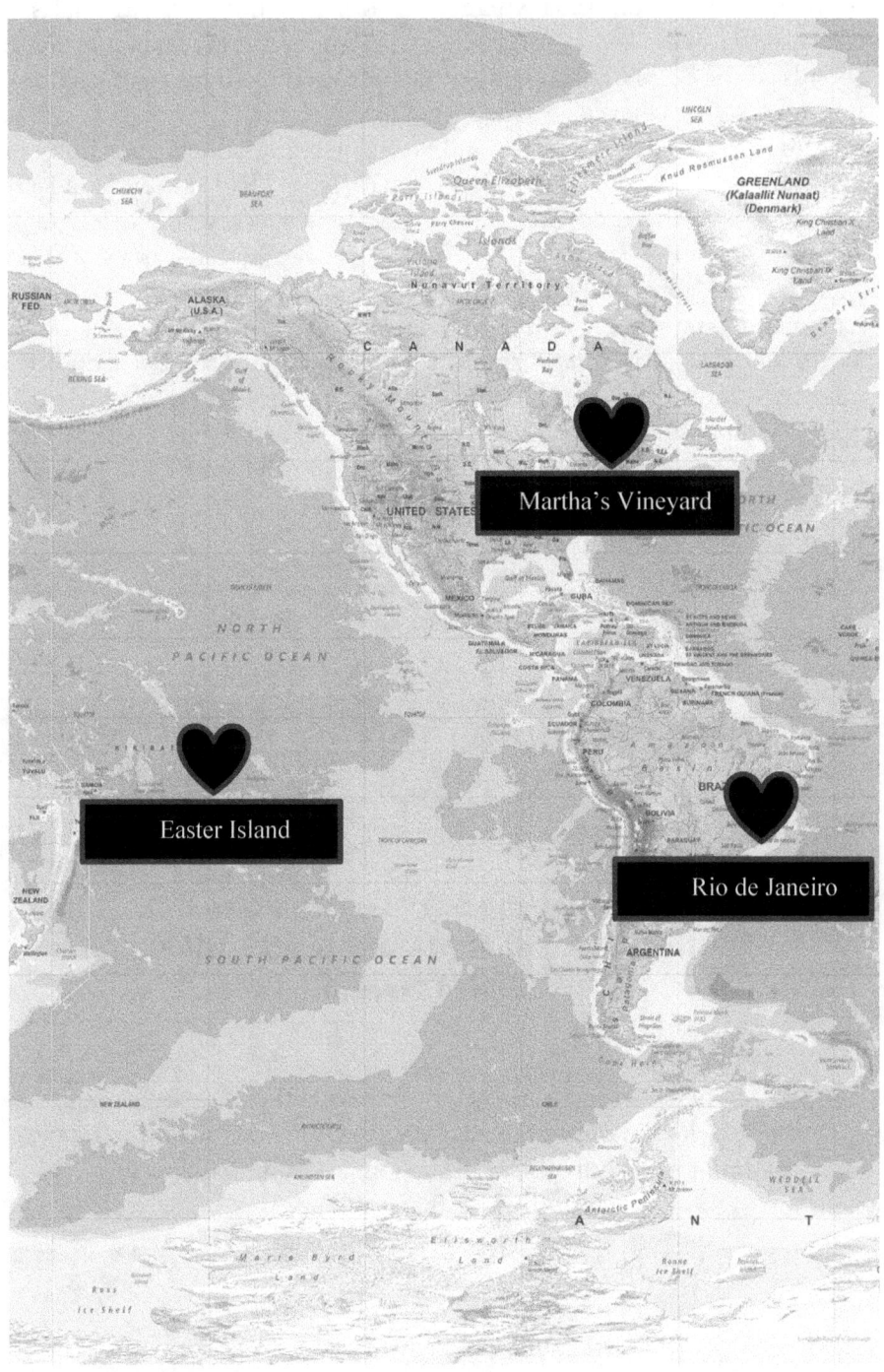

One of my vision board dreams was to move back to California where I can be near the beauty and the sounds of the ocean. During one of my morning beach walks, I had a revelation to build a business and For-Purpose organization that would serve women and girls.

I didn't know how or when it would happen, or even what it would look like, but as I've said earlier, I set the intention and made sure to stay open to all possibilities.

This meant that I had to stay spontaneous, open to my intuition, and courageous enough to act on it.

One weekend while I was visiting New York City but living in Dallas, I had the sudden impulse to put my house up for rent and move to California.

By the time I returned home a few days later, I had already found a renter. Within a week, all my belongings were in storage and I was on my way to sunny California.

I didn't doubt my decision once, because I knew something good would come of it, after all, I set the intention on my vision board.

A Real Life Example

How Following My "Get Up, Get Out and Go" Spirit Manifested a Vision Board Dream

My first year in California, I often rode the Amtrak from Los Angeles to Santa Barbara. I do my best thinking on the train, and it was during these excursions to Santa Barbara that I got the idea that I will live my dream life now… not later. Procrastination is another sign of fear. Your "get up, get out and go" spirit can lead you to life-changing moments.

Traveling Solo

The man who goes alone can start today; but he who travels with another must wait till that other is ready.
~ Henry David Thoreau

    I know. No one likes the idea of traveling alone. People feel embarrassed eating alone, going to events alone. They worry about having to make all the logistical plans by themselves. It's an understandable concern. I'm here to say that I was just like you, but I overcame my fear of traveling alone because I had places I really wanted to go.

    I couldn't wait for someone else to get their vacation time approved so they could come travel with me. I had to figure out how to travel alone and have a good time doing it. And I did.

    One of the key traits of a true "Get Up, Get Out and Go" girl is that she never meets a stranger and never lets having to travel alone deter her from a world of fun waiting just outside her doorstep. How many times have you watched a movie or read a book and recited the lines, pretending you were that character, wishing you were living that life? Stop wishing and start living it for yourself.

    This is the time. Once you master the ability to create your own joyful life, to draw experiences and people to you, you might start a vacation alone, but you'll soon find fellow adventurers, or better yet locals, who will befriend you, welcome you and make you feel right at home.

You, too, have everything you need!

I have two suggestions to help you ease into your first solo travel experience: Voluntourism, and interest-based group travel. I know what you're thinking.

"Volunteering? I'm supposed to be vacationing, not working." But when you volunteer, you may go alone but you won't be alone. You'll be interacting with people from the community, and you'll get to know the place you're visiting on a much deeper level than if you just went as a tourist.

In Cape Town, South Africa, I went to a cultural center to do some volunteer work. I participated in one of the workshops where the locals were learning how to become entrepreneurs by making and selling beautiful, artistic, ceramic bowls.

After doing this, I bought crafts from the locals and school uniforms for some of the children. That experience of volunteering taught me invaluable things that I never would have learned had I just gone as a typical tourist.

So how do you find out where to volunteer? I like to find out about a need and spontaneously serve where the need is great. I may talk to people at the hotel where I'm staying or talk to the locals about the best ways I can serve.

But there are many places you can call beforehand. You can find nonprofits or cultural centers online, call ahead of time and say you're coming for a vacation and want to spend a little time volunteering. It's that simple.

Another excellent way to travel alone without actually traveling alone is to join one of many available women's groups that offer pre-planned tours based on different interests – adventure trips, culinary trips, you name it.

You can travel with a group of other women who share similar interests to yours, which means you get to meet new people and you can start your world travel adventures without patiently waiting for your best friend or husband to get vacation time.

Structured group tours may be a great place to start.

And I really do like a four-day culinary trip in an Italian villa. You ride your bike — you know, the kind with the little bell and the cute little basket on the front — to the farmer's market, purchase your ingredients, come back and cook your meal. It's the best!

Keep your options open and be flexible. If you're like me, when I hear an Italian singing somewhere out in the countryside, I might just leave the group and be off in search of the next adventure.

The point here is not to let anything prevent you from letting your inner girl out to play, or prevent you from having the courage to create memories that will last a lifetime. Not even the fear of traveling alone, or setbacks that might occur along the way should stop you. As you'll see in the next story, not even a few skinned knees can stop me.

DISCOVER A NEW YOU, TODAY.

There is nothing more exciting than when a woman chooses to claim her worth and add value to her life.

Venice, Italy

Falling on Fifth Avenue

A Weekend Get-Away

I went for a weekend getaway to New York City to meet my girlfriend for a few days of shopping and to see a Broadway play. We had planned to have dinner that Saturday night and she and I split up for a bit to do our own thing. I decided to do some shopping on Fifth Avenue.

After visiting several stores, I had many bags in my hands, and as I went to cross the street, somehow I missed the sidewalk and fell hard.

Suddenly a large group of people flocked around me staring and asking if I was okay. I was sprawled out in the middle of a busy New York City street, not concerned at all with my fall, but instead gripping my bags tight, afraid someone might run off with them. After all, it was New York City.

Somehow I managed to get up with all my bags still in my hands. Finally, I hailed a pedi-cab – someone on a bicycle driving an open carriage – and once I settled in and set my bags down, I noticed my knees were bleeding badly. That's when they really started hurting. By the time I got to the hotel, I was limping. I had even broken my shoe strap!

You can make the best out of even the worst situation.

I finally arrived at my room, where I was met by my friend, who asked me what in the world had happened.

After I told her the story and showed her my banged-up knees, she gave me some Tylenol and bandaged me up (lucky for me, she happened to be a pediatric surgeon), and said we didn't have to go anywhere and that she was happy to stay in. "Not a chance," I said.

"I'm in New York City. We're going to dinner and seeing the play." So we went, and as we walked down the street, we laughed at the visual of me falling – me with my bruised and bloody knees insisting on having a good time, no matter what.

The next day I did hurt really badly, but I kept cracking myself up, thinking how funny I must have looked, strutting down the street like I was a Miss High Society, Breakfast at Tiffany's woman and then suddenly, there I go, falling right in the middle of the street with all my fancy bags!

The point here is that I was on one of the most sophisticated streets in the United States, but I had enough of my inner girl in me to be able to find the humor in the situation and not let it ruin my fun.

I know you have a deep desire to live your life with no regrets. To get to the end of your life and be able to say, "I lived my life with charisma, courage and spontaneity."

I'm here to remind you of that desire. And now I want you to take one more intentional step to making your life and travel dreams come true.

Whether it's Googling a hotel in one of your dream destinations and imagining yourself there, calling your girlfriend and telling her about the travel vision board you just made, or visiting an historical landmark, whatever it is, stop what you're doing, and do that one thing.

Make a decision today to make yourself a priority. Decide that you aren't going to be one of the women who thinks late in life, "what if..." and "I wish I had...," but rather, one who has fascinating stories to tell of unparalleled travels and adventures.

Journal Exercises

Journal Exercise: Visioning

Exercise One

This chapter is all about visioning — setting the intention for your wildest travel dreams and believing they will happen at the right time.

Your journal exercise here is to write about three big goals you've had that have come true for you.

It's important to do this because it will help you realize you have the power to manifest what you want, and that your dreams are closer than they appear.

Discover you.

_____

_____

_____

_____

_____

_____

_____

_____

Chapter 4: Inner Girl Issues

Real Fears.

Understandable Barriers.

As we're talking about reconnecting with your inner girl, I know this will bring up some real fears, some understandable barriers.

Throughout my travels, I meet powerful women who appear to have everything they want and need, but when we dig deeper into their childhood, we discover they've had a painful relationship with their Mom that has caused their inner girl to shut down.

Perhaps they didn't want to be poor, or to be in a dependent relationship like their Mom, so they work themselves tirelessly so they can be independent, wealthy and not have to depend on a man.

In other instances, I see women who have shut down their little girl because they were scolded by their mothers for being "irresponsible" or "silly" and told to "grow up," and act "like a lady." That playful spirit was squelched, considered insignificant and a waste of time.

Whatever the reason, all of these women had for not giving their inner girl permission to come out and play varies but, the fact is that in every area of their lives, I can see so clearly how they are making decisions in order to avoid the pain their little girl felt from being shut down by their mother.

This may not be true for every woman, but with the majority of the women I've spoken to, it boils down to the all-important mother-daughter relationship.

When your inner girl goes dormant, you lose your inner zest for life, without being aware of it and that's what happened to all these women, and may be what happened to you, too.

You end up giving your best self, your best time and energy, to things that don't truly matter to you – your job, and status symbols, like homes, cars and clothes, in order to fill the void left by the zest for life that actually needs to be filled by your inner girl's playful, adventurous spirit.

Find the time to give yourself to the people in your life who truly matter to you – and that means, first and foremost – scheduling time for your own self-care! Letting the people in your life see the lighter side of your character will open them up to the real, authentic you – the real you that is exuberant, fun and high-spirited. Your demeanor will be lighter and you will naturally be inspired to live with curiosity, charisma and courage.

I was just like you – I had children, work and a lot responsibilities. Traveling to exotic places wasn't even a thought, let alone a dream. I'd watch the Travel Channel and do a lot of wishful thinking about places I'd love to visit, but I didn't take action on my wishes.

As soon as my last child left home, I started to take my inner girl's travel dreams seriously. I wrote down my goals, and before I knew it, they manifested without me having to do much of anything besides putting myself in the right places, getting curious about life and being willing to act on my intuition and take a few risks.

In fact, after I wrote down my dreams and goals and sealed them in an envelope, I forgot all about them. I'd open the envelope a year later and discover, to my surprise, how many things had become reality for me.
I was intrigued, and began doing this exercise with everything I wanted in my life. I wrote down my ideal city and even the kind of neighbors I wanted.

I wrote down how much money I wanted to make in a year, as well as creative, entrepreneurial ideas that I wanted to turn into businesses, and all these things came true for me.

Allow yourself to experience life in a whole brave, brand new way!

As I began to get the hang of this manifestation exercise, I didn't wait for a year to pass to set new intentions. I created vision boards regularly, and would sometimes have three going at once.

Like I said in Chapter Three, my dreams would come true so quickly that I'd often end up taking down an entire board because

I had accomplished everything on it. My inner girl and I were thrilled.

I would love for you to have your own inner girl experiences everyday – to set in your mind with the powerful belief and intention that you can live courageously, whatever that looks like for you. I would love for you to discover the joy in not playing small or conforming to what's expected of you out of fear, and start reconnecting to your playful spirit by living with curiosity, charisma and courage.

There really is nothing else like it.

The most interesting and successful people take risks and live life on their own terms. They take action toward what they want to do, even if no one understands or supports them. When you have a burning desire inside your soul, don't just let it go. Keep pursuing your dreams.

The only time you really have is this moment. Start now to live your dreams and set a strong intention for what you desire to manifest. Tomorrow is not promised. Plan for it now. Take baby steps or take a big leap of faith until you can soar from the cliffs.

I went hang gliding in Hawaii because I wanted to feel what it was like to soar from a cliff. It was one of the most exhilarating and freeing things I've ever done.

You should try it, too!

If you don't know where to start, if you don't know quite how to get up, get out and go on your own, I understand. I understand that everyone is not naturally a go-getter or an extrovert.

The secret: You don't have to be.

The truth is all you have to do is simply *reconnect with your inner girl, and give her permission to come out and experience joyful living.*

I've designed some journal exercises to help you do this.

Journal Exercises

Journal Exercise: Food For Thought

Exercise One

There are good reasons why your inner girl is in time out. Unless you explore what they are, you'll just keep her there… forever.

The following questions are meant to get you thinking deeply about your inner girl and how you can rekindle that spirit.

Write and Release.

• What are the things that you're doing out of obligation that don't serve you any longer?

• Who put the idea in your head that you're obligated to do them?

• Why are you continuing to do them? What would happen if you stop?

• What are some of the things you enjoyed doing as a little girl, when time stopped and you were completely absorbed in what you were doing?

• Who were the people you enjoyed being around when you were a little girl? The people who inspired you and whom you admired?

• When did you stop doing what you love, and why? What happened that caused you to put your inner girl in the corner and leave her there?

Journal Exercise: Unleash Your Inner Girl

Write and Reflect.

Think about yourself later in life.

Will you be full of regret or grateful for the life you lived? I want to encourage you to not just make a living but to master the art of joyful living – one that radiates courage, curiosity and your inner girl's playful spirit.

But don't take my word for it.

I want to leave you with some stories of some people who have taken these concepts to heart and have been truly changed by them.

My hope is that you can understand what's truly possible in your life when you let your inner girl out to play.

The Lesson

Whatever your dreams are;
whatever memories you want to create;
wherever you want to travel,
do it!

Personal Stories

I started working with Sunnie in order to heal my anxiety and depression.

I wasn't joyful, spontaneous or playful and I wasn't taking the chances in life that I really wanted to take. But now, everything is different. I'm back to my spontaneous self.

I do what my inner girl and I are inspired to do and am not hampered by concerns about what other people might think or say about me.

It is so liberating, and I can't imagine living any other way.

And other people are noticing a difference now, too. They tell me I seem more outgoing, more joyful. And I even notice it in simple things, like in the way I dress.

I used to hide my figure behind large, loose clothes, but through your coaching, I became more confident, creative and self-expressive in my attire. In other words, my inner girl and I have a great time playing "dress-up," and I'm discovering new ways to express myself with color and fashion.

It might seem trivial, but there's a world of difference to my spirit when I walk out my front door in sweats versus a cute, colorful dress!

And all of these changes are due to me recovering and waking up my inner girl and letting her come out to play. Thank you!

T. Henderson

Sunnie, you have inspired me to be more free with myself, continue my studies and get my degree (which I never dreamed I would do!), rise out of my financial challenges, break my everyday routine and do something spontaneous, explore new horizons, and expose myself and my children to new cultures and food.

I'm like a flower that is blossoming and I love you for that.
And all of this is from you helping me connect to my inner girl, who, even now, is still trying to get out and explore, trying to get me to open up even more, be even happier than I already am.

Sunnie's influence has truly helped me transform my life.

L. Johnson

Sunnie, as I got to know you and hear how important it is to let our inner girl out to play, and as I heard story after story of how you do this so effortlessly and joyfully; how you don't let anyone cramp your style or make you apologize for pursuing your desires or for living with charisma, courage and curiosity, I began to think, *Hey, that's me. That's who I really am a free spirit.*

I live in Chicago, and when I heard stories of your Mom dancing at her favorite jazz clubs in Chicago and being such an incredible example to you of how to live the life you now do, I thought to myself, I want to be an example to my daughter—who is eight—*the way your Mom was to you.*

I want to be on fire with my life, radiant and full of joy. What makes me joyful? I asked myself. *Dancing!*

And that, my dear, is due in great part to Sunnie's powerful personality, charisma, and the potency of her stories and wisdom, all of which helped wake up my inner girl, unfurl my spirit, and bring me back to life.

Get Up, Get Out and, Go Girl!

I hope these stories have inspired you and helped you see that your inner girl spirit is the key to what you desire most. In fact, your inner girl holds the secret to the life you've always dreamed of living.

She lets you know that no matter what your challenges are, what your status is, or how many things you have, she's always ready to help you find the joy in your life. She holds the key to your charisma, curiosity and courage.

It's your little girl who knows, beyond a shadow of a doubt, that authenticity is important to a full and joyful life. I hope you are inspired to go into your heart and meet her there and let her experience life to the fullest.

One's destination is never a place, but a new way of seeing things.

Henry Miller

Thank you so much for your support. A portion of the proceeds from the sale of this book, as well as any of my programs and products, will go to support abused, abandoned and neglected girls and boys.

If this book has helped you in any way, I'd love to hear from you!

Please feel free to let me know your thoughts and testimonies by emailing me directly at sunnie@sunniegivens.com.

About the Author

Sunnie Givens is an author, transformational coach, entrepreneur, world traveler, philanthropist and a resident of the USA.

She is the founder of the Joyful Living Approach and the Joyful Living Network.

Ms. Givens is known for her ability to socialize in any environment and intuitively unleash the inner girl spirit within for almost any woman she meets.

Ms. Givens is the owner of Sunny House Inc. and the founder of The Gift Foundation, where she serves women and children of AANU (abused, abandoned, neglected and unexposed to opportunities).

For more information, visit www.sunniegivens.com.

It may be that the place you find the most special to you is closer than you think.

Dubai

In Memory of Uncle Chuck in New York

Notes

www.ingramcontent.com/pod-product-compliance
Lightning Source LLC
LaVergne TN
LVHW021407080426
835508LV00020B/2475

Living Right—
Living Well